WHISPERS
IN THE
Valley

CANDID CONVERSATIONS WITH GOD IN THE DARK

TENITA C. JOHNSON

Published by So It Is Written, LLC
Rochester, MI
SoItIsWritten.net

Whispers in the Valley: Candid Conversations with God in the Dark
Copyright © 2025 by Tenita C. Johnson

Edited by: So It Is Written – www.SoItIsWritten.net

Formatting: Ya Ya Ya Creative – YaYaYaCreative@gmail.com

ISBN: 979-8-9993606-4-9

LCCN: 2025918298

PRINTED AND BOUND IN THE UNITED STATES OF AMERICA

Table of Contents

All Things New 1

Grace for the Race 7

Ascension 13

Hidden Treasure 19

Rest 25

Peace 31

Dwell 37

Intercession 43

Letting Go 49

Mastering Peace 55

Refuge 61

Cornerstone 67

Hope Now 73

Transformation 79

Under the Blood 89

The Reshaping 91

The Shaking 97

Slowing Down 103

The Vessel 109

Full Pursuit 115

For Your Glory 121

The Portion of Peace . . 127

Valley of Darkness 133

Reset 139

The Power of Partnerships
. 145

Higher 151

Reflection 157

Never Failed 163

Solid Rock 169

Fixed Fight 175

The Plan 181

Note to Self 187

About the Author 191

All Things New

—◇◇◇—

This is the season to make room for the new! Though you may feel tired and weary, don't quit. Don't give up. Continue to ask me and believe me for the big and the great! Eyes haven't seen nor have ears heard the plans I have for you! I am about to revive all! Pursue passion but pursue purpose more! There is more to you than you know or see with the natural eye. I've planted greatness inside you for such a time as this.

Be not afraid, for I am with you. I've never left you. Never will I forsake you. You're too far from the previous shore on which you once stood to ever go back. Rest in the new. Reach for the new. As you progress, greater pieces to your purpose will be revealed! The freedom you desire is not only in forgiveness, but in total surrender. Let go of your plan to pick up mine for mine is always greater. Believe me and ask for the impossible! The more you ask, the more I can do. The more I can move. But you must ask.

Don't get ahead of me, but don't be slothful either. Keep your mind fixed on me and I will give you peace. Because I called you out of the boat, you will not sink. You will not drown. With my right hand, I will uphold you. You are great and mighty. You will do great and mighty works through me. I am your strength, your shield, your buckler. I've never lost a battle or war. I am your refuge. You can run to me and be safe. You are covered in my blood! I have hidden you for a big reveal!

You are the iceberg!

WHISPERS &
Prayer

_____

_____

_____

_____

_____

_____

_____

_____

_____

_____

_____

_____

_____

_____

_____

Grace for the Race

I am the God of more than enough. I faileth not. Just like you are blessed, your seed is blessed! I am gracing you to do more with less in this season. Don't expect to toil and strain. Cast your care upon me. There is no weight that I cannot bear. Drop the baggage. Don't carry things I have not put on you or called you to carry! Push past the frustration, past the fear and past the pain.

I am preparing the new you. Behold, I am doing a new thing. Do you not see it? Can you not know it? Expect the great! Expect the supernatural. Rest in me. Lean on me. There is safety in my arms. You are pleasing in my sight! There is greater grace for the race! Through your healing, there is great hope—not just for you—but for others. Don't let your heart wax cold. Maintain your stance in the spirit realm. Stand tall and walk boldly in that which you know I have called you to.

Eagerness is not the same as anxiety. Anxiety comes with a level of fear and torment, which is not of God! Trust me to do what I do best. This battle is already won, and the fight is fixed! Ask me for wisdom. You cannot run this race alone. Prepare to eat sweet, ripened fruit. I am making your pathway clear. I am plowing the way in which you should go. I do not bring confusion or trickery. Greater is in you than what you see, what you know and what you've heard thus far. My plans are perfect, so you don't have to be. Many are called. Few are chosen. You are both called and chosen by God!

It will be confirmed!

Ascension

I am a good, good Father. I faileth not. I'm right by your side. Every time you call out for me, I will surely answer. This season is nearing its end. Stand firm. Hold on. Better is not only coming, but it's here. Believe me and ask me for what seems impossible. Continue to train your children according to my ways. They will not fail. Your seed is abundantly blessed. Continue to praise me and worship me for what is already done!

Peace is your portion. I have planted so much more in you that is lying dormant. There is indeed a huge shift coming. Know that my plans are so much greater than what you currently know, see or fathom. You are about to see me take everything you've been through and flip the script. It's working out for the good and great.

Prepare to come up higher. Ascend in your mind. See me bigger than the things of this world. Press in closer to me to know me deeper. Expand your reach for me. Seek me for greater intimacy. As you heal, as you become more whole, you will heal others. I've redeemed you for such a time as this!

WHISPERS & Prayer

_____

_____

_____

_____

_____

_____

_____

_____

_____

_____

_____

_____

_____

_____

_____

_____

Hidden Treasure

———— ◇◈◇ ————

There is no one like me on earth. I am the one and only, true and wise God. Peace is your portion. Peace that surpasses understanding is only found in me alone. Expect to be blown away soon. The iceberg is tipping. The iceberg is flipping. I have assigned you to these mountains because I've equipped you to move them. The same power that was in Jesus when He rose from the dead rests in you.

Draw near to me and I will draw near to you. Be calm and courageous. One moment at a time. One manifestation at a time. One vision at a time. One step at a time. I've called you to tear down walls of the enemy's camp and the battle is already won. Others will be unlocked and freed through you. I'm making all things new now!

Push past fear. Push past anxiety. Push past the pain and the doubt. Rest and relax in me. You are fine. You are covered. You will know me differently and more intimately as you put one foot in front of the other. Ministry is a mandate. Your very life ministers to those who are broken and broke down.

You may not hear it. You may not see it. But as the natural seasons prepare to change, as they prepare to shift, so shall you. Remember that my plan is perfect. You have the authority to resist the enemy, and he will flee. You can speak to fear in faith, and it must cease. There is no lack in the kingdom of God. Don't stop praying. Don't stop petitioning. Launch into the deep. There is more beneath the surface. There is a treasure you have yet to unlock. Keep moving forward. Ask me, and it shall be given. New people. New places. New levels of prosperity. New levels of peace!

Ascend!

WHISPERS &
Prayer

_____

_____

_____

_____

_____

_____

_____

_____

_____

_____

_____

_____

_____

_____

_____

_____

_____

Rest

Rest in me. Abide in me. I am your God. I am your Father. With lovingkindness, I drew you. I love you. Do you not know that? I'm already on the other side of this. Speak to the mountain and it will move. All it takes is faith the size of a mustard seed. Listen to my voice. Open your eyes and ears to what I am doing now.

Expand your prophetic gift. You heard me right the first time. It's not about a title. It is about the posture of your heart. It's not just about the building, but about building people. Call me and I will answer. Praise me amid the mess. You may not know the full plan, but you know the next step. Take the next step.

I am washing you once again! I am once again cleansing you. Put your complete trust in me. Rise above the noise. I am right here. Take my hand and move forward. This will be a million-dollar year for you. Think it not strange that distractions come to sidetrack you. Trust the vision I have set before you. Cling to my very Word! Cling to my every word!

You will tread upon serpents and not be harmed. Watch, as well as pray. See yourself walking through the foyer of the new home. See yourself seated at the window seat on that airplane. The plans I have for you are gigantic! Dream bigger! Believe me for the better and greater!

WHISPERS & *Prayer*

Peace

Father God, you are gracious and merciful. I call upon you for help and healing. I cast my cares upon you. I choose to take your yoke upon me. No other help I know. I call to you, Father. I am reaching for you, Father. Father God, fear must bow to you. Anxiety must bow to you. Even this is working out for my good.

Your peace is my portion.

Whispers & Prayer

_____

_____

_____

_____

_____

_____

_____

_____

_____

_____

_____

_____

_____

_____

_____

_____

_____

_____

_____

_____

_____

_____

_____

_____

_____

_____

_____

_____

_____

_____

_____

Dwell

I am still God. I am the only wise and true God. I have already gone before you and saved you. I have already gone before you to fight your battles. You don't win the battle with physical weapons or by throwing physical darts. Stay focused on the assignment at hand. Don't lose sight of the promise I have set before you. Stand tall as the kingdom citizen I have called you to be. I am with you.

I have been, and I will continue to be. I wish above all else that you would prosper as your soul prospers. I am going before you to light the path. I am blanketing you with peace. Look to me. Don't look to the right or left. When you take your eyes off me, you lose focus of the assignment and the promise.

Many are the afflictions of the righteous, but I am right there to deliver you out of them all. Let love and grace exude from you. Do not fear man. Do not be fearful of the outcome. I am opening great, big doors that no man can shut. Lean not to your own understanding of the matter.

Trust in me with all your heart, mind and soul. There is none greater than me. I am turning it around for your good. I am flipping the script. It's not what you think. Only believe in me. Pray and believe. I faileth not. My Word will not return void. I am right there. Look for me. Reach for my presence and dwell there.

WHISPERS &
Prayer

_____

_____

_____

_____

_____

_____

_____

_____

_____

_____

_____

_____

_____

_____

_____

_____

_____

_____

_____

_____

_____

_____

_____

_____

_____

_____

_____

_____

_____

_____

_____

_____

_____

_____

_____

_____

_____

_____

_____

_____

_____

_____

_____

_____

_____

_____

_____

_____

_____

_____

 Intercession

Father God, it's me standing in the need of prayer. Father God, sometimes I don't know what to pray or how to pray. During this time and season, I need you to intercede for me. Father God, teach me your ways. Show me how to respond in love and be at peace with all men. Father God, shower your grace, your mercy, your favor, your kindness upon me. I need you more than the air I breathe and more than life itself.

Thank you for your blood that was shed. Thank you for dying for my sins. Just as you rose again, I will rise again. I will not be downtrodden or forsaken. I will not be moved or shaken by what's going on around me. Father, I call to you. No other help I know. I call to you in my times of trouble. Meet me right where I am and take me higher. Lead me to the Rock that is higher than I.

I love you, Lord. Shield me from the hands of my enemy. Break my heart for the things that break your heart. I pray for expansion and breakthrough. I pray for healing and wholeness. I pray for supernatural favor and supernatural increase. Father God, let me know that you are near and you are with me. Father God, be my peace amid the storm. You hold me in your right hand. I will not sink. I will not stumble or fall. Greater is He that is in me than he that is in the world.

Father God, I thank you for increase in my business. Saturate my life with your very presence! Let me hear only your voice so clearly!

WHISPERS & Prayer

_____

_____

_____

_____

_____

_____

_____

_____

_____

_____

_____

_____

_____

_____

_____

_____

_____

_____

_____

_____

_____

_____

_____

_____

_____

_____

_____

_____

_____

_____

_____

_____

_____

_____

Letting Go

*H*ave you not heard? Strength! Courage! Boast only in me and the goodness of me. I've called you to greater. Come up higher. I sit high and I look low. There is none like me. Continue to seek me and you will indeed find me. I have redeemed you from the hand of the enemy. I have already conquered death, hell and the grave. Nothing will by any means consume you. Nothing will harm you by any means. Remain steadfast and unmovable. You may bend, but I promise you won't break.

Some of your best days are on the other side of this. Your best days are ahead of you. They are in front of you. Forget that which is behind you. Forget the people. Forget the places. Forget the things that it seems you have lost. Let love and grace abound. But where I'm taking you, some people can't go. Anxiety can't go. Fear can't go. There is a glory cloud resting upon you and your household. The enemy has no authority. When he sees the blood of Jesus on you, he must pass over. I am not only *with* you, but I am *in* you, moving for you and through you. This is your greatest time to shine. As darkness seems to increase around you, shine brighter. Press in harder. Seek me more. Praise me more. Worship me more. I've never lost a battle. I've never lost a war! You have already won!

WHISPERS & *Prayer*

_____

_____

_____

_____

_____

_____

_____

_____

_____

_____

_____

_____

_____

_____

_____

_____

Mastering Peace

———— ◈◈ ————

This is the season when the seed of greatness which I have planted within you shall spring forth. Eyes have not seen, nor has it entered the hearts of man that which I am about to do for you and through you. Stand boldly in that which I have called you to and that which I called you to do.

Rest in me. Find peace in me. Master your peace. Once you find the place of peace, fight to keep it with all your might. Don't stop dreaming. Awaken your dreams that are lying dormant. Dream again. Believe boldly again. I am a faithful Father and I faileth not. When have I ever let you fall? I carry you. I've got you and I've got this.

Speak to the storm, and it will cease! Cast your cares. Cast them onto my shoulders. I am the great burden bearer. You will not be taunted or tormented! The enemy has no power over you! He is already defeated. He is under your feet. I am right here. Look for me. Reach for me. Feel for me. Test me and see if I won't come through for you!

I am God!

There is none above me!

WHISPERS & Prayer

Refuge

ather God, I need you! God, I'm growing weary and tired yet again. I need your strength. I need your love. I need you to wrap your loving arms around me. I know that I am free and free indeed. I press toward the mark of the high calling. Father God, show yourself strong. Show up and show out in my life like you have done so many times before. Heal me, and I shall be healed. Save me, and I shall be saved.

Father, I repent for making decisions without consulting you. I repent for every mistake and for every time I got ahead of you. I repent for every ill word spoken against your people. Father God, I pray for greater wisdom, favor, grace and mercy. Give me a heart like yours. Give me the mind you want me to have. Cause me to think higher thoughts and not get caught up in the earthly trials of life. Carry me in those times when the boat of life gets shaky. Help me to see myself as you see me. Help me to see myself on the other side of the mountain. God, I run to you for safety.

You are my place of refuge.

WHISPERS & Prayer

_____

_____

_____

_____

_____

_____

_____

_____

_____

_____

_____

_____

_____

_____

_____

_____

_____

_____

_____

_____

_____

_____

_____

_____

_____

_____

_____

_____

_____

_____

_____

_____

_____

_____

Cornerstone

— ◈◈ —

The joy of the Lord is my strength. I will yet praise you, Lord. God, I need you more than life itself. I need your glory. I need your mercy and grace. Pour out your favor upon me. Pour out blessings so bountiful that I do not have room to receive. Show yourself strong in my life. Open my eyes to see you crystal clear. Open my ears to hear you clearly. Train my eyes and ears to always see and hear what you are doing.

I cast my cares upon you. This weight has seemed too great to bear. Since I have sowed and because I have seed in the ground, I know you will do the exceedingly, abundantly above all I could ask or think. Peace comes to me now. Joy comes to me now. Happiness is coming to me now. God, make my next steps plain. Make my next movement plain.

God, I trust you. God, I adore you and worship you for your goodness and your glory. Guide and direct me. Guide and direct me as I steward my time and talents. Make my feet like hindsfeet. Make me steadfast and unmovable. You are my *only* hope. You are my *only* refuge.

You are my cornerstone.

I don't want to simply exist. It is now time to truly *live*!

WHISPERS & *Prayer*

Hope Now

od, my God, you have called me to set the captive free. You have called me out of darkness into your marvelous light. You have called me to open blind eyes and deaf ears. You have called me to be a beacon of light amid what seems bleak and hopeless. Your Spirit lies within me, that same spirit that raised Jesus from the dead. So, help me to remember you are with me and you are for me, even when it doesn't seem like you are moving or working.

Father God, I call upon you for strength. I call upon you for perfect peace. I call upon you to show yourself strongly in this season. Father God, I trust in you. But help my areas of unbelief when it seems nothing is happening. God, no other help I know. Where else shall I go? Where else can I turn? Who else can I look to for help? None other than you.

When my heart is troubled, speak to my heart. When my mind is racing, calm my troubled mind. I will yet hope now in God! I will yet stand on His words and His promises.

Father God, I thank you that your plans are to give me hope and a future of abundance. I thank you that your plans are not to harm me in any way.

Thank you for doing the exceedingly, abundantly above all I can ask or think. I praise you for being the one and only, true and wise God. I thank you that when I am weak, you carry me. Thank you for loving me when I didn't love myself. Thank you for rescuing me from the hands of my enemies. Thank you for shining your face upon me and calling me out of a life of darkness!

WHISPERS &
Prayer

_____

_____

_____

_____

_____

_____

_____

_____

_____

_____

_____

_____

_____

_____

_____

_____

_____

_____

_____

_____

_____

_____

_____

_____

_____

_____

_____

_____

_____

_____

_____

_____

_____

_____

Transformation

———— ◇◇ ————

God, my God, you are faithful. You are righteous. You are holy. There is no one like you. No one cares like you, and no one compares to you. Thank you for showing up for me once again, like you always have. Thank you for showering your love and peace upon me. Thank you for awakening the dead areas of my life. Thank you for the grace to trust you more when I don't see you and when I don't feel you.

Great is thy faithfulness to me forevermore! Father God, if you take care of the birds of the air and the animals of the field, how much more will you take care of me? How much more will you shower upon your children. Open my ears to hear. Open my eyes to see you in all that I do.

Don't let me miss you because you appear in an unfamiliar form. I worship you from the depths of my heart and soul. Transform me into the woman of God you have called me to be. Mold me into the ambassador of Christ you have called me to be. More than anything, let me complete the assignments you have set before me. Let me serve as a beacon of light and hope where others see hopelessness. Pour out your Spirit afresh upon me. Let me know and experience you in a different way. Bring back to my remembrance your many promises.

_____

_____

_____

_____

_____

_____

_____

_____

_____

_____

_____

_____

_____

_____

_____

_____

_____

_____

_____

_____

_____

_____

_____

_____

_____

_____

_____

_____

_____

_____

_____

_____

Under the Blood

Father God, you have come to my rescue once again! Thank you for being my rock, my cornerstone, during times of uncertainty. Thank you for stability. Thank you that I am experiencing overflow in my life, family and business. Thank you that you always cover me. You always shelter me. You uphold me with your right hand. Thank you for being my place of refuge. Thank you for your grace and mercy continually following me all the days of my life.

God, you cover and wash me.

I am under your blood!

WHISPERS &
Prayer

The Reshaping

You are my child, in whom I am well pleased. I have called you to uproot and plant, to build and to set things in motion. Prepare to be used mightily in the kingdom. Remember that you are the hands and feet of Jesus. You represent me on earth. Strength! Courage! Love! Boldness! I have called you to shake up traditions of men that do not line up with my Word.

Follow my example. Follow my lead. Listen to my voice and my instructions. Let love and grace abound. Be quick to offer mercy and be quick to forgive. Be quick to love, not show judgement. Seek me for wisdom and strategy in all things. Ask me for that which seems to be impossible.

I am reshaping your mind and heart in this season. Be sensitive to what is going on around you. You have the power to shift atmospheres. You have the power to decree and declare a thing, and it shall be. I'm right here. I haven't left. I haven't gone silent on you. I have not forsaken you. I've hidden you for such a time as this.

Prepare for the big reveal. Prepare to be introduced to the new you. I am God, and I make all things new. I'm yet remaking, reshaping and rebuilding. Behold, I'm doing a new thing. Can you not see it? Do you not know it? Can you not perceive it?

It's happening quickly, fast and easy!

Be encouraged!

WHISPERS & Prayer

The Shaking

od, you are great! You do miracles so great. Father God, thank you for the overflow and abundance. Mold me and shape me. Teach me how to manage your wealth you have given me to steward. Make me a manifestation of your presence. Make me a manifestation of your glory. Make me a masterpiece of miracles. There is more! There is so much more!

God let me know and see what it feels like to be slain in the spirit and overcome with your presence! Make me an atmosphere shifter. Shift through me. Change others through me. Pour out yourself onto others through me. Break my heart for the things that break your heart.

You can trust me with the wealth. You can trust me with the souls. You can trust me with the assignment. Make my life like that of a lighthouse during darkness in the land. Thank you for the boldness and the strategy to pursue purpose and passion. Thank you for allowing me to weather every storm. Thank you for making me steadfast and unmovable. Cause me to see you and know you in deeper depths, heights, lengths and widths!

I accept the assignment, even when I don't know the totality of it all. Create in me a clean heart, oh God, and renew a right spirit within me.

Thank you for the shift. Thank you for the shaking!

WHISPERS &
Prayer

_____

_____

_____

_____

_____

_____

_____

_____

_____

_____

_____

_____

_____

_____

_____

_____

_____

Slowing Down

⸻ ◇◇ ⸻

Father God, you are gracious, and you are merciful. You are my only hope, my chief cornerstone. You are my pillar of peace. Father God, speak through me. Use me to unlock the broken and the captive. Use me to prophesy and edify your body. Use me to teach, to transform and to build. Activate the apostolic mantle and calling you have placed upon me. Give me clarity and boldness to walk into all you have for me. Give us wisdom and discernment on how to move your kingdom forward! Give us greater financial wisdom and greater stewardship over the things you call us to manage.

Help us to slow down long enough to hear you and be led by you!

WHISPERS & *Prayer*

The Vessel

Father God, incline my ear to hear you clearly. Open my eyes to see you moving and working in all situations. Take this heart of stone and turn it to a heart of flesh. Infuse hope and empowerment into me so that I can pour into others! Train my ears and eyes to notice you first before I see or hear it from a natural standpoint!

Meet me right where I am. Mold me and shape me into the vessel that you can pour new wine into. Strengthen my prophetic gift and help me exercise every gift you have seeded into me. Let faith and patience rise within me! Thank you for the millions and the billions you have released to me so that I may pour into your kingdom. Use my hands and feet to heal, to bind and to loose. Thank you for choosing me. Thank you for loving me even when I didn't see value in myself.

Make me a vessel through which your blessings flow! Amen!

WHISPERS & Prayer

Full Pursuit

———— ◇◇ ————

I will use you mightily. Trust my heart when you cannot see my hand. I am still God. There will be no other gods before me. I have poured out my spirit upon you for a time such as this. The standard is love. The response is love. The cure is love. The way is love. Incline your ear to hear.

Open your eyes to see greater. Ask me for wisdom and you will be made wise. Ask me for greater revelation and I will reveal. Continue to be steadfast and unmovable! You ain't seen nothing yet! Prepare for the big! Prepare to shift! I am with you always! I planted you in the earth for purpose with purpose! Pursue and recover all! That which you cannot reach I am granting you access!

WHISPERS &
Prayer

_____

_____

_____

_____

_____

_____

_____

_____

_____

_____

_____

_____

_____

_____

For Your Glory

ather God, I thank you that you make rivers in the desert and streams in desolate wastelands. Thank you for making a way amid the times where there seems to be no way. Help me to remove the boulders that are blocking the constant flow of abundance that I know you've called me to experience. Help me to remove the muck and mire, the mud, the pebbles and the stones. Take my stony heart and turn it into a heart of flesh.

Remove every form of blockage and hindrance that is keeping me from experiencing the fullness that you have intended for me and my family. God, use me for your glory and for your mighty works. Make me a beacon of your love and light, your hope and your healing, your majesty and your glory! Though it tarry, I will patiently wait for it. I will continue to believe I will see the goodness of the Lord in the land of the living!

WHISPERS & *Prayer*

The Portion of Peace

———⟨◇⟩———

Father God, I pray you encamp your angels around me and my family. Please give us wisdom and revelation as to how it relates to your Word to be God-led parents! Thank you for your grace and mercy you give us daily! Please restore our hope. Restore our faith. Restore our vision to see our children as you see them. Help us to guide them as you see them in the spirit realm. I declare and I decree that peace is our portion, and we speak to the storm to cease in the name of Jesus!

WHISPERS & Prayer

_____

_____

_____

_____

_____

_____

_____

_____

_____

_____

_____

_____

_____

_____

_____

_____

Valley of Darkness

---◇◇◇---

Thank you, Lord, that even though I have felt confused and in the dark, your hand will guide me and your strength will support me. Thank you, Lord, that even though I have felt unwanted and unplanned, you say every moment of my life was laid out before a single day had passed. You saw me before I was born.

Thank you, Lord, that even though I sometimes am afraid of what the future does or does not hold, your Word says that you go before me and follow me. Thank you, Lord, that even though I may feel I am in a valley of darkness, I can never escape from your Spirit. I am never without your presence!

WHISPERS & Prayer

_____

_____

_____

_____

_____

_____

_____

_____

_____

_____

_____

_____

_____

_____

_____

Reset

Father God, I need you more than I've ever needed you before. Father God, this is new, and I don't understand what's happening. Help me to see through your lens. Show forth your mighty hand and your mighty power! Reset us and revive us. Help me to know you in a brand-new way. Father God, reveal your plan, your ways, your path for this season. Teach me how to love the way in which you love! I won't be moved by what I see. I won't be moved by what I hear. I won't be shaken, and I won't be moved by things in the natural. Let your power fall upon me afresh. Transform me from the inside out. Create in me a clean heart, oh God! Bless me, indeed!

WHISPERS & Prayer

_____

_____

_____

_____

_____

_____

_____

_____

_____

_____

_____

_____

_____

_____

_____

_____

_____

_____

_____

_____

_____

_____

_____

_____

_____

_____

_____

_____

_____

_____

The Power of Partnerships

———◇◇◇———

*F*ather God, I thank you for sending me accountability partners who want to do the work and won't look at the assignment as just another thing to do. Thank you that just like I am accountable to you, me and my accountability partner will be excited about speaking daily and connecting daily.

Thank you that we will download creative ideas amongst each other to better each other's business. Thank you for sending me someone who will uplift, uphold and strengthen me. Thank you for the power and the authority that comes when two or three are gathered in your midst. Father God, thank you that I am not a burden or a bother to anyone. I thank you for strategic partnerships, divine destiny intersections and overflow in my business and relationships!

WHISPERS & Prayer

_____

_____

_____

_____

_____

_____

_____

_____

_____

_____

_____

_____

_____

_____

_____

Higher

Father God, I thank you that your Word says when I am weak, you are strongest. Father, I am weak. Show yourself strong. Father God, when I am faint, I thank you that you will uphold me with your right hand. Father, I pray for your divine wisdom, revelation and power.

Fill me up so I can pour into your people. Father God, pour out fresh revelation and oil upon me. God, I don't want to teach out of my own will and desires! I submit my agenda and my will to your perfect plan and will. Father God, cause me to come up higher and see higher than what is going on in the earth!

WHISPERS & *Prayer*

_____

_____

_____

_____

_____

_____

_____

_____

_____

_____

_____

_____

_____

_____

_____

Reflection

————— ◇◇◇ —————

Father God, thank you that you clothe me in righteousness and favor. Thank you for sending the increase in quality clientele who not only value my work, but don't mind paying for my services in full. Thank you for the tenacity and the boldness to run with the vision and plan you've given me. God, make your perfect plan crystal clear. I yield my plan to your perfect will and plan. Take control. I surrender all my plans and desires to yours. Father God, show me the missing pieces. Show me what I need to change and what I need to do differently. Let your perfect will be done through me and to me! May I continue to reflect your love and light!

WHISPERS & *Prayer*

_____

_____

_____

_____

_____

_____

_____

_____

_____

_____

_____

_____

_____

_____

Never Failed

———⬦⬦———

Father God, I need you! You are the Lord of lords and King of kings. Thank you for your unfailing love and kindness to me. God, make my assignments crystal clear in this season. Bring new wine out of me. Unlock gifts within that have lied dormant for years and use them for your glory!

Make a way in this wilderness, Lord! Father God, I thank you that all things work together for my good! Help me to forgive those who have walked away, ghosted me or hurt me. God, heal my heart and mind! Father God, thank you for my million-dollar year! Thank you that this is the year I get clarity on the ministry in the marketplace you have called me to tend! You've never failed us, and you won't start now! Thank you that this will be a transformational year!

WHISPERS & *Prayer*

Solid Rock

I'm right here, daughter! I haven't left you! I am right here! Rest in me! Abide in me! You are beautiful! You are fearfully and wonderfully made. Rest. Relax. Reset. Recalibrate. Trust me. My way is better! For I know the plans I have toward you, plans of hope and a future! My plan is greater! Remember that I waste nothing! Think it not strange the season that you're in! If Christ is your firm foundation, if I am your firm foundation, you are unshakable and unbreakable as you stand firm on the solid rock!

WHISPERS &
Prayer

_____

_____

_____

_____

_____

_____

_____

_____

_____

_____

_____

_____

_____

_____

Fixed Fight

*I*t's not coming the way you think. Faith doesn't make things easy. It makes them possible. Find the place of rest and peace in me that I have for you. Believe me for the radical and the ridiculous! No matter what it looks like in the natural, believe for bigger. Never get complacent where you are with me. I am not coming the same way twice. Someone new is knocking on your door. Let go of one rope to grab hold of the next one. Be not afraid and don't lean to your own understanding. The victory is yours. The fight is fixed.

WHISPERS & *Prayer*

The Plan

God, I feel like I am in a perpetual state of grief. I need you now more than ever. I love you with my whole heart, God. You are great, kind and merciful! God, reach in and heal my heart from the inside out. I know you to be the mind regulator, the heart mender and heart fixer, the lover of my soul. God, please be my place of refuge. Be my hope where there seems to be no hope. Be my rock and firm foundation when everything around me is shaking.

Be my shield. Guard me and hide me under your almighty wings. Prepare my heart and mind for the days, the weeks and the months ahead. Guide me and direct my path. Help me to stay on the path of righteousness and purpose. God, I don't know what to do or where to go next. Help me not to move out of emotion, fear or hopelessness. I don't want to move outside of your will.

God, I look to you for my purpose, my validation, my hope, my stability. You're my only living hope. If you don't come, God, it won't be done. Hold my hand and hold my head up when I am downtrodden. Rescue me in despair! Rescue me from my own unbelief and self-sabotage! God, I know you are in the details. You're in the waiting. You're in the silence. Help me to rest in you. Help me to stand firmly in you. Help me to know that you are God and God alone. No other help I know. God, there is no plan B. You are my plan. Help me to know you are near!

WHISPERS & Prayer

_____

_____

_____

_____

_____

_____

_____

_____

_____

_____

_____

_____

_____

_____

_____

_____

Regardless of what people say or don't say to you, God calls you royalty. He calls you redeemed, healed and whole. You have been set free from the bondage of the opinions of man. You are worthy of love, peace and joy. But always remember that God is your firm foundation. All other ground is sinking sand. You cannot please people. Seek ye first the kingdom of God and everything else will be added to you. You are beautiful because you are made in the image of God. Love unapologetically and dream big!

There are God-sized dreams inside you! Unlock and unleash them!

WHISPERS & *Prayer*

About the Author

───────◇◇───────

*T*ransforming pain into purpose is a gift that authorpreneur, speaker and book coach, Tenita "Bestseller" Johnson gives to everyone she encounters. She is a warrior of words with a fierce passion for guiding authors to expand their brand by showing them how to earn multiple streams of income from just ONE book. As the author of 26 books, eight of which have been Amazon bestsellers, she is living proof that sharing your story leads to your destiny.

Familiar with rising from numerous fires and coming out unscathed, Tenita has triumphed over suicidal thoughts, depression, low self-esteem, marital storms and blended family woes. She also endured miscarriages and the loss of twins just the day after she married her husband. Each of these tragedies added indelible layers to her resilience. With more than 25 years in journalism, writing and editing, she has a knack for creating narratives that are authentic and raw, yet endearingly relatable. She is a vessel with the ability to change lives and impact the world, thus she is known as the proud "book bully," who relentlessly urges others to, "Write the book and get paid for the pain!"

When Tenita speaks, people listen with their ears as well as their hearts and souls because her transparency transcends pretense. She is a bold beacon of hope who inspires others to seek their highest peak. One of her proudest and defining moments was her appearance on Kirk Franklin's Praise Sirius XM channel for her book, *HUSH: Breaking the Cycle of Silence Around Sexual Abuse.*

As the founder and CEO of So It Is Written, she has helped hundreds of authors birth their books in record time. The company excels as a one-stop shop for the complete book process from conception to completion. The editorial guru successfully helps people to pen books that will boost their brand, accelerate their paydays and bust open doors of endless opportunities. So It Is Written received The Sunrise Pinnacle Award for Diversity Company of the Year from the Rochester Regional Chamber of Commerce and has been nominated for several awards for the Troy Chamber of Commerce.

Beyond her books, her versatility shines in multiple areas, including her role as the executive producer of the hit stage play, *When the Smoke Clears*, which was based on her book, *When the Smoke Clears: A Phoenix Rises*. The play ran in 2017, 2018 and 2024 to sold-out audiences in downtown

Detroit at the Boll YMCA Theatre. In addition, Tenita serves as a board member and ambassador for the Troy Chamber of Commerce.

Tenita's passion for delivering bestselling books is matched only by her devotion to helping women and men heal from the trauma and baggage of sexual abuse. *HUSH: Breaking the Cycle of Silence Around Sexual Abuse* features both men and women who lost their innocence and identity to sexual abuse. She is a huge advocate and mouthpiece for those who have been sexually abused as she empowers them to release their pain instead of suffering in silence.

Her plans include producing her short film *What Happens in This House* and producing her full feature film *When the Smoke Clears*. As a catalyst for positive change, she is a woman who has learned to live an intentional life of purpose while unapologetically fulfilling her God-driven assignments.

For booking or speaking engagements, email info@soitiswritten.net or visit www.tenitajohnson.com.